Simple FABRIC FOLDING *for Christmas*

14 FESTIVE QUILTS & PROJECTS

LIZ ANELOSKI

C&T PUBLISHING

© 2003 Liz Aneloski
Editor: Lee Jonsson
Technical Editor: Franki Kohler
Copyeditor: Annette Bailey
Proofreader: Carol Barrett
Cover Designer: Kris Yenche
Book Designer: Dawn DeVries Sokol
Design Director: Diane Pedersen
Illustrator: Tim Manibusan
Production Assistant: Kirstie L. McCormick
Quilt Photography: Sharon Risedorph
How-To Photography: Kirstie L. McCormick and Diane Pedersen
Set Photography: Diane Pedersen and Kirstie L. McCormick
Published by C&T Publishing, Inc., P.O. Box 1456, Lafayette, California 94549

Front cover: *Christmas Tree—All Dressed Up Quilt* and *Folded Eight-Pointed Star Pillow*
Back cover: *Wrapped Up and Under the Tree Quilt* and *Can't Wait 'till Christmas Calendar*

Library of Congress
Cataloging in Publication Division
101 Independence Ave., S.E.
Washington, D.C. 20540-4320

Library of Congress Cataloging-in-Publication Data

Aneloski, Liz
  Simple fabric folding for Christmas : 14 festive quilts & projects /
Liz Aneloski.
      p. cm.
Includes index.
  ISBN 1-57120-202-1 (Paper trade)
  1. Patchwork--Patterns. 2. Origami. 3. Quilting. 4. Christmas
decorations. I. Title.
  TT835 .A4937 2003
  746.46--dc21

                         2002014663

Printed in China
10 9 8 7 6 5 4 3 2 1

Contents

Dedication

To my family, whose support and encouragement mean more to me than they will ever know;

and to Gramma, the shining star who watches over all of us.

Acknowledgments

I would like to thank:

Mary Mashuta for giving me my first fabric folding experience with origami squares;

Rebecca Wat for showing me there is a wonderful world of fabric folding;

and Alex Anderson for being so supportive and encouraging during the process of creating my first book.

Introduction and Tips

This creative journey began with encouragement from my family and was followed by support from C&T Publishing. I hope you will find these projects fun to fold and stitch, as well as beautiful additions to your holiday decorating and gift-giving.

Be creative and have fun choosing your fabrics. Most of the ones I used are not Christmas-themed fabrics; they are a variety of reds and greens that can be purchased any time of year. Just remember that the fabrics you see in the projects will not be available when this book actually reaches the store shelves. Choose fabrics you love and you will be thrilled with your creations.

- Use a good-quality fabric for folding foundations for the origami puffs. Spray-starch and iron the fabric before cutting. You will use each foundation several times, so make sure it will hold its shape in order to give you an accurate finished unit. Press the foundation after each use. Continue to use each foundation until it doesn't hold its shape when pressed.

- Press the seam allowances away from the folded units.

- You may use a fat quarter where a ⅛ yard fabric requirement is given.

- Use glass-head pins so you can press over them without melting the heads.

- Use a seam ripper or stiletto to hold folded corners in place while pressing so you don't burn your fingers.

- Press with steam to set the folds.

Single Tucks

½" Tucks

1. Cut a strip the size specified in the project instructions. Trim off the selvages. Place the fabric right side up. Starting 1" from one short edge, draw lines on the right side of the fabric along the entire length, using a gridded ruler (1" apart for ½" tucks and 1½" apart for ¾" tucks). Be sure the lines are 90° to the long raw edges of the fabric.

2. With the fabric placed vertically, wrong side up, fold the top edge toward you to align the first two lines.

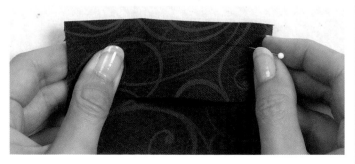

3. With the wrong sides together, line up the two lines, creating a fold. Insert a pin into the top layer directly on the line at one end.

4. Then adjust the line on the bottom layer so the pin exits right on the line.

5. Bring the pin back up through the top layer, on the line, to hold the two layers. Continue to pin along the line. Leave approximately ½" between the pins.

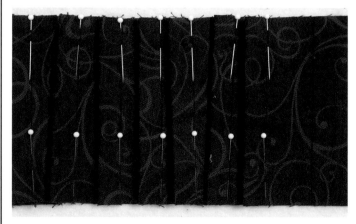

6. Fold and pin, using the same process, along the entire length of the fabric. You may have an extra line at the end if you started with an odd number of lines. It doesn't matter because you will trim this to the length specified in the project instructions.

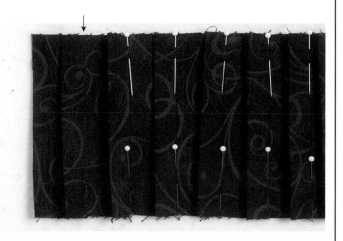

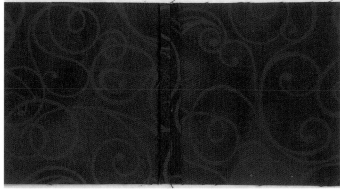

7. Stitch on the first pinned line. Remove each pin just as the sewing machine needle approaches. Stitch on each pinned line.

1. Cut 2 strips of fabric the size specified in the project instructions. Trim off the selvages. With right sides together, stitch the 2 strips together along one short edge. Press the seam open.

8. With the right side up, center the fold on the seam line.

2. Place the fabric right side up. Draw a line on the right side of the fabric, ¼" to the left of the seam line, using a gridded ruler. Be sure the line is 90° to the long raw edges of the fabric. Mark this line with a pin.

9. Press each tuck flat.

3. Work from this line and draw lines 1½" apart along the entire length of the fabric.

4. Follow Steps 2–9 on pages 6–7 to pin, stitch, and press.

DoubleTucks

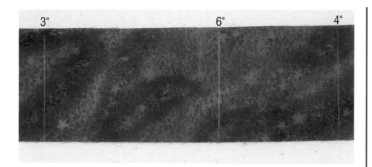

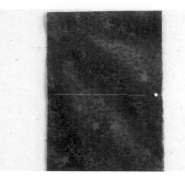

1. Cut a strip the size specified in the project instructions. Trim off the selvages. Place the fabric right side up. Draw a line 3" from one end using a gridded ruler. Draw a line 6" from the first line. Then draw a line 4" from the last line. Continue drawing lines, alternating 6", 4", and so on to the end of the strip. Be sure the lines are 90° to the long raw edges of the fabric.

4. Bring the pin back up through the top layer directly on the line to hold the two layers.

2. With the fabric placed vertically, wrong side up, fold the top edge toward you to align the first two lines, creating a fold. Insert a pin into the top layer directly on the line at one end of the line.

5. Continue to pin along the line. Leave approximately ½" of space between the pins. Fold and pin using the same process (matching the lines that are 6" apart), along the entire length of the fabric.

3. Then adjust the line on the bottom layer so the pin exits right on the line.

6. Stitch on the first pinned line. Remove each pin just as the sewing machine needle approaches. Stitch on each pinned line.

7. Draw a line 1" from the first fold. Be sure the line is 90° to the raw edges of the fabric.

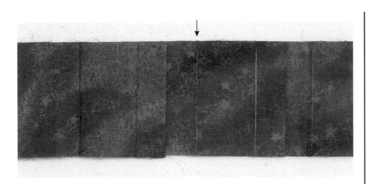

8. Stitch on the drawn line. You can skip Step 7 and just stitch 1" from the fold, but be sure you stitch very straight and exactly 1" from the fold so your tucks will be straight.

9. With the right side up, align the fold on top of the seam lines.

10. Press the tucks flat. Repeat for each fold.

Traditional Prairie Point

1. Cut a square of fabric the size specified in the project instructions. Place the fabric wrong side up.

2. Bring the two top corners to meet the two bottom corners and fold the rectangle in half. Press. Finger-press to mark the center of the top folded edge.

3. Bring one top corner to meet the bottom edge at the finger-pressed mark. Press.

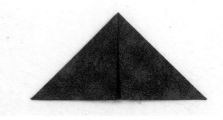

4. Bring the other top corner to meet the bottom edge at the finger-pressed mark to form a point. Press.

Prairie Point with Fold

1. Cut a rectangle of fabric the size specified in the project instructions. Place the fabric wrong side up with the longer sides on the sides and the shorter sides on the top and bottom.

2. Bring the two top corners to meet the two bottom corners and fold the rectangle in half. Press.

3. Fold the folded edge down ¼". Press.

4. Turn the fabric over so the ¼" fold is underneath. Finger-press to mark the center of the top folded edge.

5. Bring one top corner to the bottom edge at the finger-pressed mark. Press.

6. Bring the other top corner to the bottom edge at the finger-pressed mark to form a point. Press.

Simple Pocket

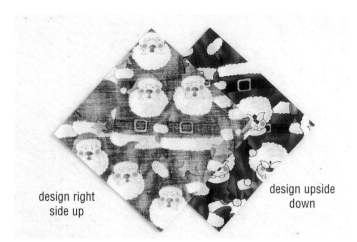

design right
side up

design upside
down

1. Cut two squares of fabric the size specified in the project instructions. Place the squares right sides together. *If you are using a printed fabric with a design that has a direction, make sure the design is right side up on one square and upside down on the other square. When the corner flops down, the design will be right side up.*

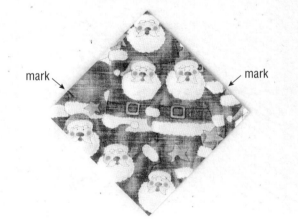

mark

mark

2. On the square with the design right side up, make a mark on the two top edges ¾" from the side corners.

3. Using a ¼" seam allowance, begin stitching at one mark, backstitch to secure the threads, and continue stitching along one side. Pivot at the corner, continue stitching along the second side to the second mark, and backstitch.

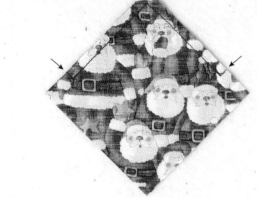

4. Clip the seam allowances at the marks to within two threads of the stitching. Clip the stitched corner to reduce the bulk so you get a nice square corner.

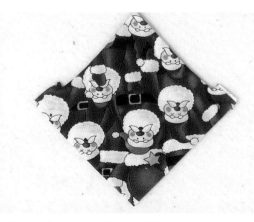

5. Turn the pocket right side out. Make sure the unstitched sections of the seam allowance are visible. Press.

Pocket with Fold

1. Cut a square of fabric the size specified in the project instructions. Place the fabric wrong side up.

2. Bring the top corner to meet the bottom corner and fold the square in half. Press.

3. Fold the folded edge down ¼". Press.

4. Turn the fabric over so the ¼" fold is underneath. Finger-press to mark the center of the top folded edge.

5. Bring one top corner to the bottom corner at the finger-pressed mark. Align the raw edges.

6. Bring the other corner to the bottom corner at the finger-pressed mark to form a point. The tails of the folded corners will hang down past the bottom corner. Press.

7. Trim off the folded corners that hang past the bottom corner.

Square Origami Puff

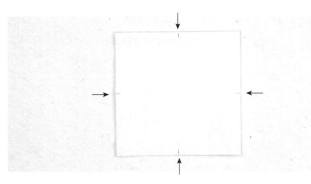

1. Cut a square of fabric for the foundation the size specified in the project instructions. Mark the center of each edge. (It doesn't matter if you mark the right or wrong side of the fabric.)

2. Cut a colored square the size specified in the project instructions. Place the colored square, right side up, on top of the unmarked side of the foundation square. Match one corner of the foundation square to one corner of the colored square and place a pin diagonally across the corner. Repeat for the remaining three corners.

3. Starting at one corner, smooth the edge of the colored square to match the edge of the foundation square, just to the mark. Place a pin to hold the two layers of fabric together at the mark.

4. On the other end of the same edge, smooth the edge of the colored square to match the foundation square along the remainder of the edge, forming a pleat. Pin through all the layers to hold the pleat in place. Remove the first pin.

5. Rotate the square and repeat Steps 3 and 4 for the remaining three sides. Be sure to fold each pleat the same direction.

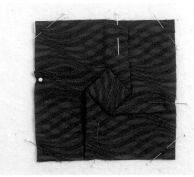

6. Gently manipulate the fabric with your fingers to form the center square. Press. Remove the pins and the foundation square. Baste the pleats.

Triangle Origami Puff

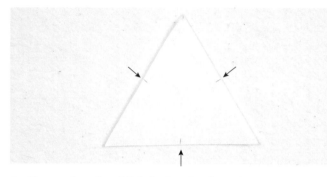

1. Cut a triangle of fabric for the foundation the size specified in the project instructions. Mark the center of each edge. (It doesn't matter if you mark the right or wrong side of the fabric.)

2. Cut a colored triangle the size specified in the project instructions. Place the colored triangle, right side up, on top of the unmarked side of the foundation triangle. Match one corner of the foundation triangle to one corner of the colored triangle and place a pin diagonally across the corner. Repeat for the remaining two corners.

3. Starting at one corner, smooth the edge of the colored triangle to match the edge of the foundation triangle, just to the mark. Place a pin to hold the two layers of fabric together at the mark.

4. On the other end of the same edge, smooth the edge of the colored triangle to match the edge of the foundation triangle along the remainder of the edge, forming a pleat. Pin through all the layers to hold the pleat in place. Remove the first pin.

5. Rotate the triangle and repeat Steps 3 and 4 for the remaining two sides. Be sure to fold each pleat the same direction.

6. Gently manipulate the fabric with your fingers to form the center. Press. Remove the pins and the foundation triangle. Baste the pleats.

Rectangle Origami Puff

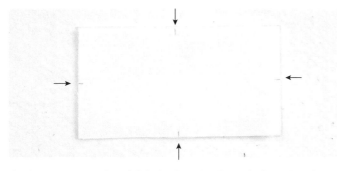

1. Cut a rectangle of fabric for the foundation the size specified in the project instructions. Mark the center of each edge. (It doesn't matter if you mark the right or wrong side of the fabric.)

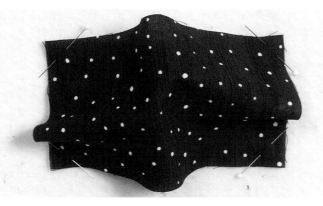

2. Cut a colored rectangle the size specified in the project instructions. Place the colored rectangle, right side up, on top of the unmarked side of the foundation rectangle. Match one corner of the foundation rectangle to one corner of the colored rectangle and place a pin diagonally across the corner. Repeat for the remaining three corners.

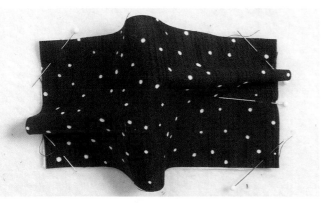

3. Starting at one corner, smooth the edge of the colored rectangle to match the edge of the foundation rectangle on one edge, just to the mark. Place a pin to hold the two layers of fabric together at the mark.

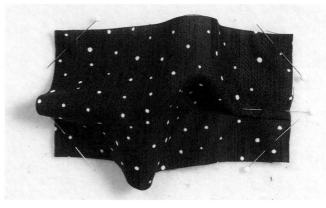

4. On the other end of the same edge, smooth the edge of the colored rectangle to match the edge of the foundation rectangle along the remainder of the edge, forming a pleat. Pin through all the layers to hold the pleat in place. Remove the first pin.

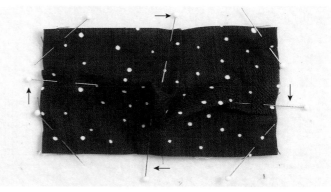

5. Rotate the rectangle and repeat Steps 3 and 4 for the remaining three sides. Be sure to fold each pleat the same direction.

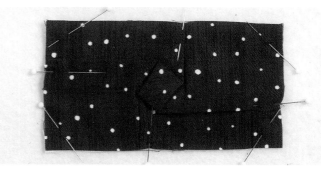

6. Gently manipulate the fabric with your fingers to form the center. Press. Remove the pins and the foundation rectangle. Baste the pleats.

Folded Square

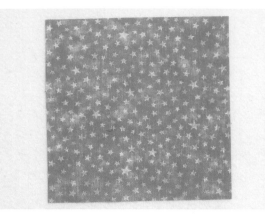

1. Cut a square of fabric the size specified in the project instructions. Place the fabric wrong side up.

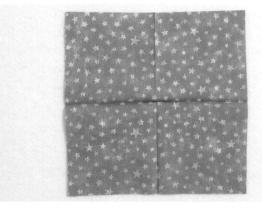

2. Fold the square in half horizontally. Press. Open the square and fold in half vertically. Press. Open the square. The intersection of the pressed lines marks the center.

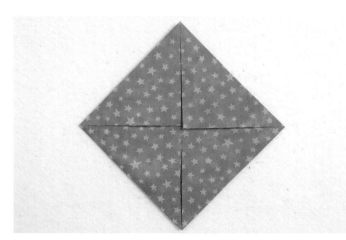

3. Bring each of the four corners to meet exactly at the center of the square. Smooth to be sure the corners are even and flat. Press. (It is more important for the corners to be perfect than for the points to meet in the center.)

4. Turn the square over (folded side down).

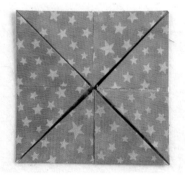

5. Bring each of the four corners to meet exactly at the center of the square. Smooth to be sure the corners are even and flat. Press. (It is more important for the corners to be perfect than for the points to meet in the center.)

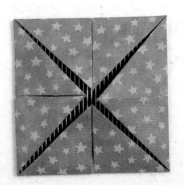

6. Cut a fabric insert the size specified in the project instructions. Open the center points and place the fabric insert in position. The center points will be brought to the outside edge of the square and tacked down after the square is stitched into the project.

Folded Eight-Pointed Star

1. Cut a square of fabric the size specified in the project instructions. Place the fabric wrong side up.

2. Bring the top corner to meet the bottom corner and fold the square in half. Press.

3. Open the square.

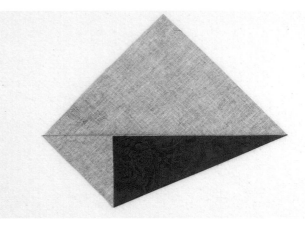

4. Bring the lower right edge of the square to the fold line. Press.

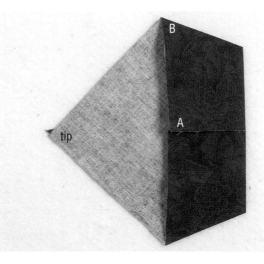

5. Bring the upper right edge of the square to the fold line. Press.

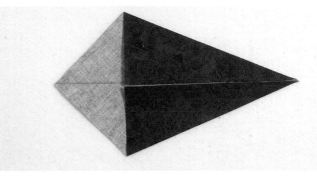

6. Bring the right corner underneath and match this right corner to the left corner. Press.

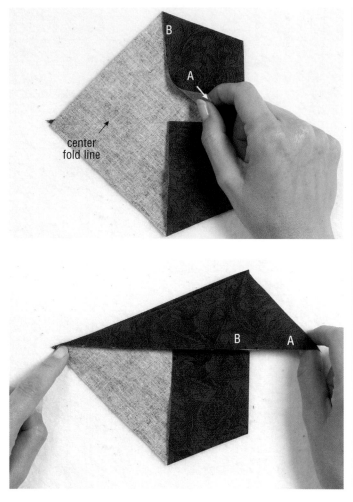

center fold line

9. Repeat to fold the bottom section out.

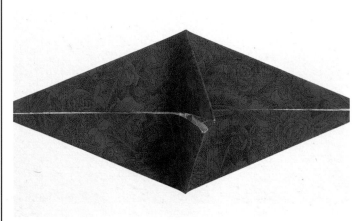

7. Pick up A and pull it out to open the top section. B will come down to meet the center fold line.

10. Open the underneath layers out.

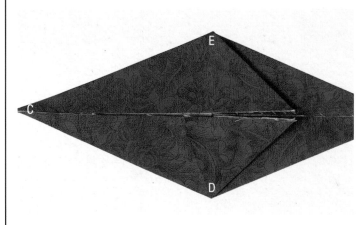

11. Press with the small center flaps to the right.

8. Press.

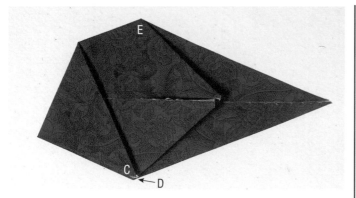

12. Bring C down to D. Press.

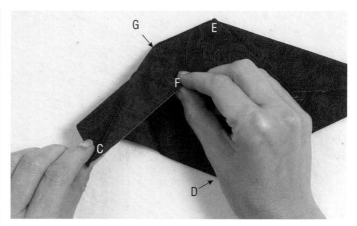

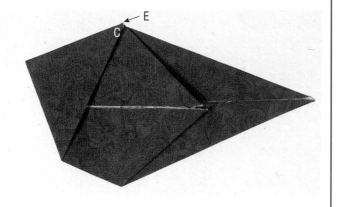

13. Open C and bring it up to E. Press.

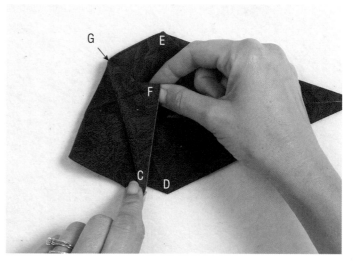

15. Pull F out with your thumb and bring C down to D.

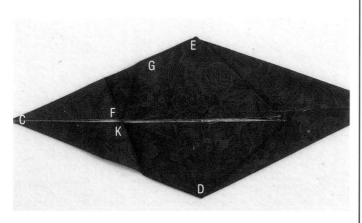

14. Open C back up.

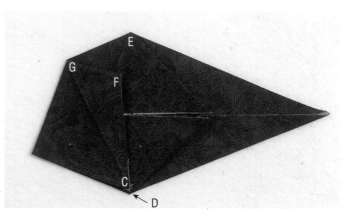

16. Fold on the fold line between F and G. Press.

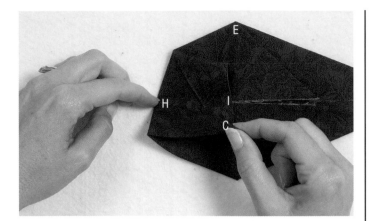

19. Pull J out and open out the section underneath the folds.

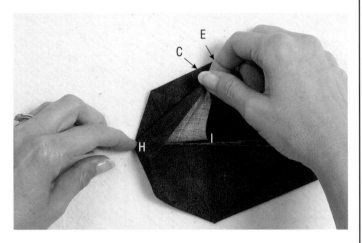

17. Bring C up to E, creating a fold from H to I.

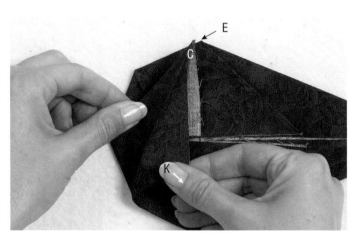

20. Put J back into its previous place and bring C to E.

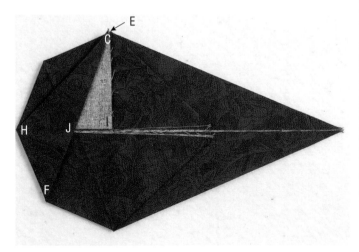

18. Press.

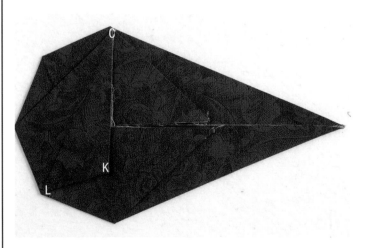

21. Bring C up to E, creating a fold between K and L. Press.

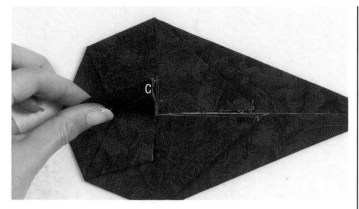

22. Bring C up so it sticks straight up.

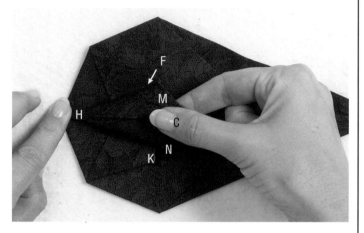

23. Put your index finger inside this flap and push down with your thumb to open the flap.

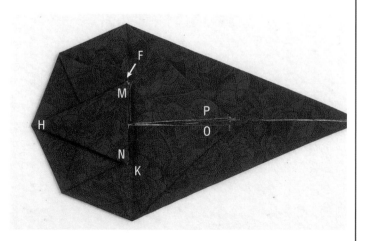

24. Fold the flap flat so M meets F, N meets K, and a point is folded at H. Press.

25. Tuck C underneath the top layer of fabric, creating a fold between M and N. Press.

26. Fold points O and P to meet H. Press.

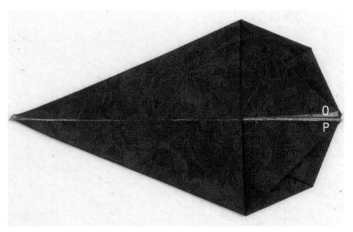

27. Rotate 180°.

28. Repeat Steps 11–25. Rotate 90° counter-clockwise.

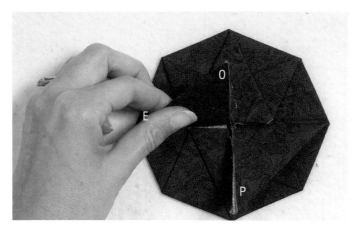

29. Bring O up so it sticks straight up.

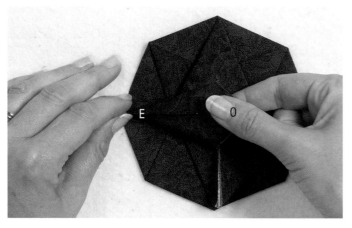

30. Put your thumb inside this flap and push down with your index finger to open the flap.

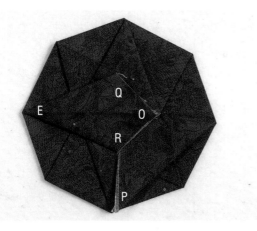

31. Fold the flap flat so the fold line down the center of this flap aligns with the fold line on flap P and a point is folded at E. Press.

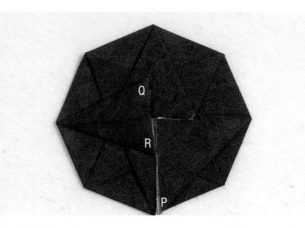

32. Tuck O underneath the top layer of fabric, creating a fold between Q and R. Press.

33. Fold P the same way you just folded O.

34. Arrange the triangle points in the center so they alternate over, under, over, under. Press.

A·Country·Christmas·

Wrapped Up and Under the Tree Quilt

MATERIALS

Yardage is based on 42" fabric width.

■ ⅞ yard of plaid for packages and outer border
■ ⅜ yard each of 8 green prints for trees
■ ⅜ yard each of 8 red prints for tree backgrounds
■ ⅛ yard of brown print for tree trunks
■ ⅜ yard for folding foundations
■ ¼ yard of dark blue print for inner border
■ 1¼ yards for backing
■ ½ yard of red/gold print for binding
■ 45" x 41" batting
■ 96 gold beads (5mm)
■ ¼ yard for hanging sleeve

CUTTING

Always remove selvages.

Plaid

- Cut 2 strips 6" x fabric width. From these strips, cut 9 squares 6" x 6" for packages.
- Cut 4 strips 3½" x fabric width for outer border. (Trim to size later.)

Green Prints

- Cut 1 rectangle 12" x 10½" from each of the fabrics (8 total) for large trees. (Trim as shown.)
- Cut 2 rectangles 6" x 5½" from each of 7 of the fabrics and 1 rectangle 6" x 5½" from the eighth fabric (15 total) for small trees. (Trim as shown.)

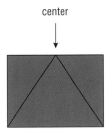

center

Trim from center of top (long) edge to corner, on both sides.

Red Prints

- Cut 2 rectangles 4¾" x 8¼" from each of the fabrics for the large tree backgrounds (16 total). *The 2 layers of fabric for these 2 rectangles must be placed wrong sides together before cutting.* Cut in half diagonally. (You will have leftover triangles but you have to cut this way or half of your triangles will be backward.)
- Cut 2 rectangles 1½" x 3½" from each of the fabrics for the large tree backgrounds (16 total).
- Cut 4 rectangles 2¾" x 4¾" from each of 7 of the fabrics and 2 rec-

tangles 2¾" x 4¾" from the eighth fabric for the small tree backgrounds (30 total). Cut in half diagonally. (See note for red triangles left.)

- Cut 4 rectangles 1" x 2" from each of 7 of the fabrics and 2 rectangles 1" x 2" from the eighth fabric used above for the small tree backgrounds (30 total).

Brown Print

- Cut 1 strip 1½" x fabric width. From this strip cut 8 rectangles 1½" x 2½" and 15 rectangles 1½" x 1" for the tree trunks.

Foundations

- Cut 2 squares 4½" x 4½" for packages.
- Cut 2 rectangles 8⅞" x 7¾" for large trees. (Trim as shown left.)
- Cut 4 rectangles 4⅞" x 4¼" for small trees. (Trim as shown left.)

Dark Blue Print

- Cut 4 strips 1½" x fabric width for inner border. (Trim to size later.)

Red/Gold Print

- Cut 5 strips 2¼" x fabric width for binding.

Hanging Sleeve

- Cut 1 strip 8" x fabric width for hanging sleeve. (Trim to size later.)

FOLDED UNITS

- Make 9 Square Origami Puffs following the instructions on page 13.
- Make 8 large and 15 small Triangle Origami Puffs following the instructions on page 14.

CONSTRUCTION

Use ¼" seam allowance.

TREE BLOCKS

Use matching background fabrics for each tree.

1. Place a background triangle on top of a tree triangle with right sides together, aligning the top corners. Stitch. Press.

2. Repeat for the other background triangle.

Align top corners and stitch.

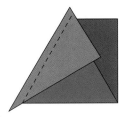

Add other background triangle.

3. Stitch a background rectangle to each side of a tree trunk. Press.

4. Stitch this unit to the tree unit. Press. Make 8 large tree blocks and 15 small tree blocks.

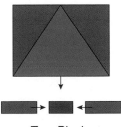

Tree Block

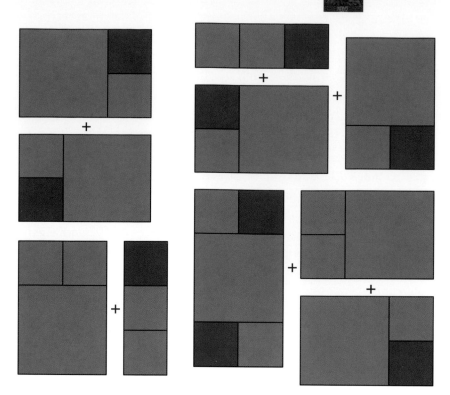

Stitch together in sections.

TOP

1. Arrange the blocks as shown in the illustration.

2. Stitch the blocks into sections. Press.

3. Stitch the sections together. Press.

BORDERS

Your top should measure 32½" x 28½". If it does, follow the instructions below and trim the border strips to the lengths specified. If it doesn't, see page 62 for how to measure and trim the border strips to fit your top.

Inner Border

1. Trim 2 of the inner border strips to 28½" long. Stitch them to the sides. Press.

2. Trim the other 2 inner border strips to 34½" long. Stitch them to the top and bottom. Press.

Outer Border

1. Trim 2 of the outer border strips to 30½" long. Stitch them to the sides. Press.

2. Trim the other 2 outer border strips to 40½" long. Stitch them to the top and bottom. Press.

FINISHING

QUILTING

1. Layer and baste following the instructions on page 62.

2. Stitch in-the-ditch around the blocks, trees, and borders. Then quilt around the center triangles of the large trees. I quilted around 1⅝" star stickers (purchased at a craft store) in the backgrounds of the large trees and the outer border, and around 1" star stickers in the backgrounds for the small trees.

EMBELLISHMENT

Stitch 12 beads to the background of each large tree.

BINDING

1. Add binding following the instructions on pages 62–63.

2. Add a hanging sleeve following the instructions on page 63.

3. Be sure to add a label to your Christmas heirloom.

Quilt Construction

WRAPPED UP AND UNDER THE TREE
TABLE RUNNER AND PLACEMATS

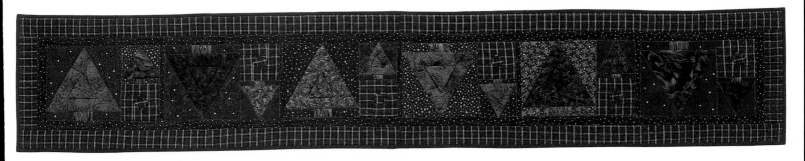

MATERIALS

Yardage is based on 42" fabric width. These requirements are for one table runner OR six placemats.

- ⅝ yard of plaid for packages and outer border of table runner OR 1 yard for placemats
- ⅜ yard each of 6 green prints for trees
- ¼ yard each of 6 red prints for tree backgrounds
- 1½" x 22" scrap of brown print for tree trunks
- ⅜ yard for folding foundations
- ⅜ yard of dark blue print for inner border and dividing strips of table runner OR ½ yard for inner border of placemats
- 1⅝ yards of backing for table runner OR 2 yards for placemats
- ½ yard of red print for table runner binding OR ⅞ yard for placemat binding
- 19" x 85" batting for table runner OR 6 pieces 19" x 23" for placemats
- 72 beads (5mm)

CUTTING

Always remove selvages.

Plaid

- Cut 1 strip 6" x fabric width. From this strip, cut 6 squares 6" x 6" for packages.

FOLDING TECHNIQUES
- Square Origami Puffs
- Triangle Origami Puffs

TABLE RUNNER
- 81" x 14½"
- 8" and 4" finished blocks

PLACEMAT
- 18½" x 14 ½"
- 8" and 4" finished blocks

- Cut 5 strips 2½" x fabric width for outer border of table runner. Stitch 2 of these strips into a long strip. From this strip, cut a strip 81". Repeat for 2 more of the strips for top and bottom outer borders of table runner. From the remaining strip, cut 2 strips 10½" long for the side outer borders of the table runner.

OR

- Cut 10 strips 2½" x fabric width for the outer border of the placemats. From one of the strips, cut 2 strips 18½" long for the top and bottom outer borders. Repeat for 5 more of the strips (12 total 18½" strips). From one of the remaining strips, cut 3 strips 10½" long for the side outer borders. Repeat for 3 more strips (12 total 10½" strips).

Green Prints
- Cut 1 rectangle 12" x 10½" from each of the fabrics (6 total) for the large trees. (Trim as shown.)
- Cut 1 rectangle 6" x 5½" from each of the fabrics (6 total) for the small trees. (Trim as shown.)

center

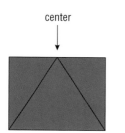

Trim from center of top (long) edge to corner on both sides.

Red Prints
- Cut 2 rectangles 4¾" x 8¼" from each of the fabrics for the large tree backgrounds (12 total). *The 2 layers of fabric for these 2*

rectangles must be placed wrong sides together before cutting. Cut in half diagonally. (You will have leftover triangles but you have to cut this way or half of your triangles will be backward.)

- Cut 2 rectangles 1½" x 3½" from each of the fabrics for the large tree backgrounds (12 total).
- Cut 2 rectangles 2¾" x 4¾" from each of the fabrics for the small tree backgrounds (12 total). Cut in half diagonally. (See note for red triangles above.)
- Cut 2 rectangles 1" x 2" from each of the fabrics for the small tree backgrounds (12 total).
- Cut 6 strips 2¼" x fabric width for the table runner binding.

OR

- Cut 12 strips 2¼" x fabric width for placemats.

Brown Print
- Cut 6 rectangles 1½" x 2½" and 6 rectangles 1½" x 1" for the tree trunks.

Foundations
- Cut 1 square 4½" x 4½" for the packages.
- Cut 1 rectangle 8⅞" x 7¾" for the large trees. (Trim as shown left.)
- Cut 1 rectangle 4⅞" x 4¼" for the small trees. (Trim as shown left.)

Dark Blue Print
- Cut 2 strips 1" x fabric width. From these strips, cut 5 strips 8½" long for table runner dividing strips.
- Cut 5 strips 1½" x fabric width for inner border of table runner. Stitch 2 of these strips into a long strip. From this strip, cut a strip

77". Repeat for 2 more of the strips for top and bottom inner borders of table runner. From the remaining strip, cut 2 strips 8½" long for side inner borders of table runner.

OR

- Cut 9 strips 1½" x fabric width for inner border of placemats. From 1 of the strips, cut 2 strips 14½" long for the top and bottom inner borders of placemats. Repeat for 5 more of the strips (12 total 14½" strips). From 1 of the remaining strips, cut 4 strips 8½" long for the side inner borders of placemats. Repeat for 2 more strips (12 total 8½" strips).

FOLDED UNITS

- Make 6 Square Origami Puffs following the instructions on page 13.
- Make 6 large and 6 small Triangle Origami Puffs following the instructions on page 14.

CONSTRUCTION
Use ¼" seam allowance.

TREE BLOCKS
Use matching background fabrics for each tree.

1. Place a background triangle on top of a tree triangle with right sides together, aligning the top corners. Stitch. Press.

2. Repeat for the other background triangle.

Align top corners and stitch.

Add other background triangle.

3. Stitch a background rectangle to each side of a tree trunk. Press.

4. Stitch this unit to a tree unit. Press. Make 6 large tree blocks and 6 small tree blocks.

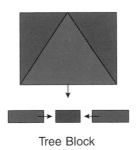

Tree Block

TOP

1. Arrange the blocks and dividing strips (for table runner) as shown in the illustrations.

2. Stitch the blocks together. *Notice that the folded square/small tree sections are on the left side of half of the large trees and the right side of the other half of the large trees.* Press.

BORDERS

Your top should measure 75" x 8½" OR 12½" x 8½". If it does, follow the instructions below and trim the border strips to the lengths specified. If it doesn't, see page 62 for how to measure and trim the border strips to fit your top.

Inner Border

1. Stitch an 8½" strip to each short side of either the table runner OR each placemat. Press.

2. Stitch the two 77" strips to the top and bottom of the table runner OR stitch two 14½" strips to the top and bottom of each placemat. Press.

Outer Border

1. Stitch a 10½" strip to each short side of either the table runner OR each placemat. Press.

2. Stitch the two 81" strips to the top and bottom of the table runner OR stitch two 18½" strips to the top and bottom of each placemat. Press.

FINISHING

QUILTING

1. Layer and baste following the instructions on page 62.

2. Stitch in-the-ditch around the blocks, trees, and borders. Then quilt around the center triangles of the large trees. I quilted around 1⅝" star stickers (purchased at a craft store) in the backgrounds of the large trees and the outer border, and around 1" star stickers in the backgrounds for the small trees.

EMBELLISHMENT

Stitch 12 beads to the background of each large tree.

BINDING

Add binding following the instructions on page 62–63.

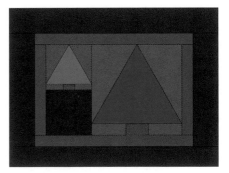

Placemat Construction

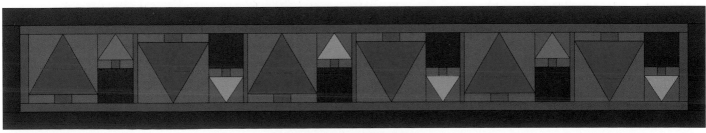

Table Runner Construction

FOREST OF TREES STOCKING

FOLDING TECHNIQUE

■ Traditional Prairie Points

STOCKING

■ 8" x 16"

■ 2" finished blocks

MATERIALS

Yardage is based on 42" fabric width.

■ ¾ yard of plaid for the dividing strips, binding, hanger, backing, and lining

■ 13 scraps 2½" x 3½" of green prints for the trees

■ ⅛ yard each of 6 red prints for the tree backgrounds and prairie points

■ 1½" x 18" scrap of brown print for the tree trunks

■ 24" x 20" batting

CUTTING

Always remove selvages.

Plaid

■ Cut 2 strips 2½" x fabric width for dividing strips. From these strips, cut 2 strips 2½" x 8½", 1 strip 2½" x 11", and 1 strip 2½" x 10". From the remainder, cut 1 strip 1½" x 8½" and 1 strip 1½" x 10".

■ Cut 1 strip 2¼" x fabric width for binding and hanger.

■ Backing and lining will be cut later.

Green Prints

■ Cut 13 rectangles 2¼" x 3" for the trees. (Trim as shown.)

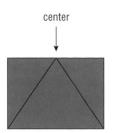

center

Trim from center of top edge
to corner, on both sides.

Red Prints

- Cut 2 squares 3" x 3" from each of 5 of the fabrics and 3 squares 3" x 3" from the 6th fabric for prairie points (13 total).
- Cut 4 rectangles 1¾" x 2¾" from each of 5 of the fabrics and 6 rectangles 1¾" x 2¾" from the 6th fabric for the small tree backgrounds (26 total). *The two layers of fabric for these two rectangles must be placed wrong sides together before cutting. Cut in half diagonally. (You will have leftover triangles but you have to cut this way or half of your triangles will be backward.)*
- Cut 4 rectangles 1" x 1¼" from each of 5 of the fabrics and 6 rectangles 1" x 1¼" from the 6th fabric used above for the small tree backgrounds (26 total).

Brown Print

- Cut 13 squares 1" x 1" for tree trunks.

FOLDED UNITS

- Make 13 Traditional Prairie Points following the instructions on page 9.

CONSTRUCTION

Use ¼" seam allowance.

TREE BLOCKS

Use matching background fabrics for each tree.

1. Place a background triangle on top of a tree triangle, with right sides together, aligning the top corners. Stitch. Press.

2. Repeat for the other background triangle.

Align top corners and stitch.

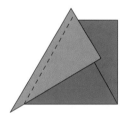

Add other background triangle.

3. Stitch a background rectangle to each side of a tree trunk. Press.

4. Stitch this unit to a tree unit. Press. Make 13 tree blocks.

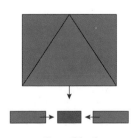

Tree Block

STOCKING FRONT

1. Baste the overlapping prairie points to the top edge of 3 of the 2½" dividing strips.

2. Using the illustration as a guide, stitch the tree blocks into rows. Press.

3. Trace and complete the stocking pattern on page 61.

4. Arrange the tree, prairie point rows, and 1½" dividing strips, adjusting the placement so they completely cover the pattern.

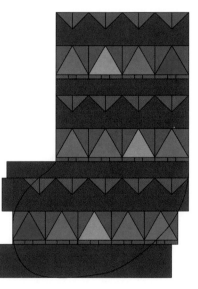

Adjust the rows to cover the pattern.

5. Stitch the rows together. Press.

6. Cut out the stocking using the pattern.

7. Place the lining fabric wrong side up. Lay the batting on top of the lining with the stocking front right side up on top of the batting. Baste the layers together.

8. Stitch in-the-ditch between the rows.

9. Trim around the stocking to remove the extra batting and lining.

STOCKING BACK

1. Layer the backing, wrong side up; the batting and the lining, right side up. Baste the layers together.

2. Quilt as desired.

3. Using the stocking front as a pattern, cut out the stocking back.

FINISHING

FINISHING TOUCHES

1. With right sides together, stitch the stocking together, leaving the top edge open.

2. Make the folded binding strip following the instructions on page 63 (Step B). Trim off an 18" piece of the folded strip for the binding and an 8" piece for the hanger.

3. Open the 8" piece and fold long raw edges to meet at center fold line. Fold in half along center fold line. Topstitch along both folded edges.

4. Fold the 8" piece for the hanger in half, matching raw edges. Stitch the binding onto the top edge of the stocking, inserting the hanger (on the inside of the stocking) into the seam allowance.

5. Hand stitch the binding to the inside of the stocking, leaving the

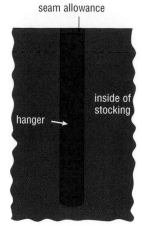

Insert the hanger into
the binding seam allowance.

hanger hanging down inside the stocking.

6. Bring the hanger up and hand-stitch to secure in position.

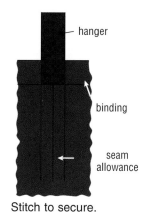

Stitch to secure.

Stocking Construction

A Fun Christmas

CANDY CANES AND FOLDED FLYING GEESE QUILT

MATERIALS

Yardage is based on 42" fabric width.

- 2⅛ yards of red print #1 for prairie points, outer border, and binding
- ¾ yard of plaid for prairie point backgrounds and border corners
- ½ yard of small red-and-white stripe for prairie point blocks
- ½ yard of white print for folded eight-pointed stars
- ¼ yard of red print #2 for folded eight-pointed star backgrounds
- ¼ yard of large red-and-white stripe for inner border
- 1⅜ yards for backing
- 43" x 49" batting
- ¼ yard for hanging sleeve

CUTTING

Always remove selvages.

Red Print #1

- Cut 8 strips 4" x fabric width. From these strips, cut 72 squares 4" x 4" for prairie points.
- Cut 8 strips 3½" x fabric width for outer borders. (Trim to size later.)
- Cut 5 strips 2¼" x fabric width for binding.

Plaid

- Cut 5 strips 4½" x fabric width. From these strips, cut 72 rectangles 2½" x 4½" for the prairie point backgrounds.
- Cut 4 squares 3½" x 3½" for the border corners.

Small Red-and-White Stripe

- Cut 2 strips 6½" x fabric width. From these strips, cut 24 rectangles 2½" x 6½" for blocks.

White Print

- Cut 2 strips 8½" x fabric width. From these strips, cut 6 squares 8½" x 8½" for folded eight-pointed stars.

Red Print #2

- Cut 1 strip 6½" x fabric width. From these strips, cut 6 squares 6½" x 6½" for folded eight-pointed star backgrounds.

Large Red-and-White Stripe

- Cut 4 strips 1½" x fabric width for inner border. (Trim to size later.)

Hanging Sleeve

- Cut 1 strip 8" x fabric width for hanging sleeve. (Trim to size later.)

FOLDED UNITS

- Make 72 Traditional Prairie Points following the instructions on page 9.
- Make 6 Folded Eight-Pointed Stars following the instructions on pages 17–22.
- Make 4 outer borders with ¾" Tucks Using Two Strips of Fabric following the instructions on page 7.

CONSTRUCTION

Use ¼" seam allowance.

PRAIRIE POINT BLOCKS

1. Baste a prairie point to a prairie point background rectangle. Make 72 units.

2. Stitch 3 of the above units into a section. Press. Make 24 sections.

3. Stitch a small red-and-white striped rectangle to a prairie point section as shown. Press. Make 24 blocks.

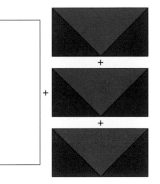

Stitch sections and add rectangle.

FOLDED EIGHT-POINTED STAR BLOCKS

Appliqué a folded eight-pointed star to a red print #2 square. Make 6 blocks.

TOP

1. Arrange the blocks as shown in the illustration.

2. Stitch the blocks into rows. Press away from the folded edges as much as possible.

3. Stitch the rows together. Press away from the folded edges as much as possible.

BORDERS

Your top should measure 30½" x 36½". If it does, follow the instructions below and trim the border strips to the lengths specified. If it doesn't, see page 62 for how to measure and trim the border strips to fit your top.

Inner Border

1. Trim 2 of the inner border strips to 36½" long. Stitch them to the sides. Press.

2. Trim the other 2 inner border strips to 32½" long. Stitch them to the top and bottom. Press.

Outer Border

1. Trim 2 of the tucked outer border strips to 38½" long. *When you trim the single tucked border strip, adjust where you cut to allow an untucked section for the seam allowance. Remove the stitching of 1 tuck if necessary.*

2. Stitch them to the sides. Press.

3. Trim the other 2 tucked outer border strips to 32½" long. *See note in Step 1.*

4. Stitch a border corner to each end of these 2 strips. Press. Stitch them to the top and bottom. Press.

FINISHING

QUILTING

1. Layer and baste following the instructions on page 62.

2. Stitch in-the-ditch around the blocks, sections, units, and around the folded eight-pointed stars.

EMBELLISHMENT

Tack the tucks as shown right.

FINISHING TOUCHES

1. Add binding following the instructions on pages 62–63.

2. Add a hanging sleeve following the instructions on page 63.

3. Be sure to add a label to your heirloom.

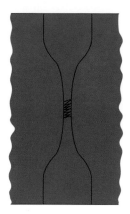

Tack the tucks.

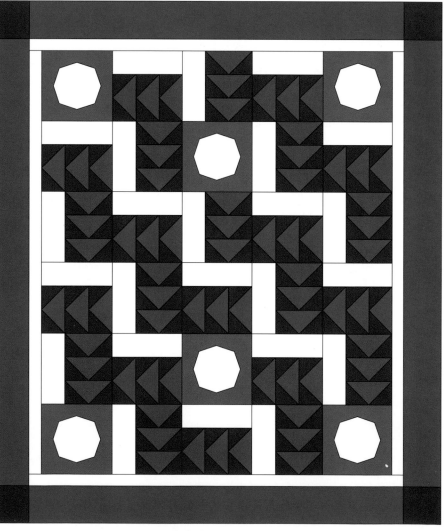

Quilt Construction

CAN'T WAIT 'TIL CHRISTMAS CALENDAR

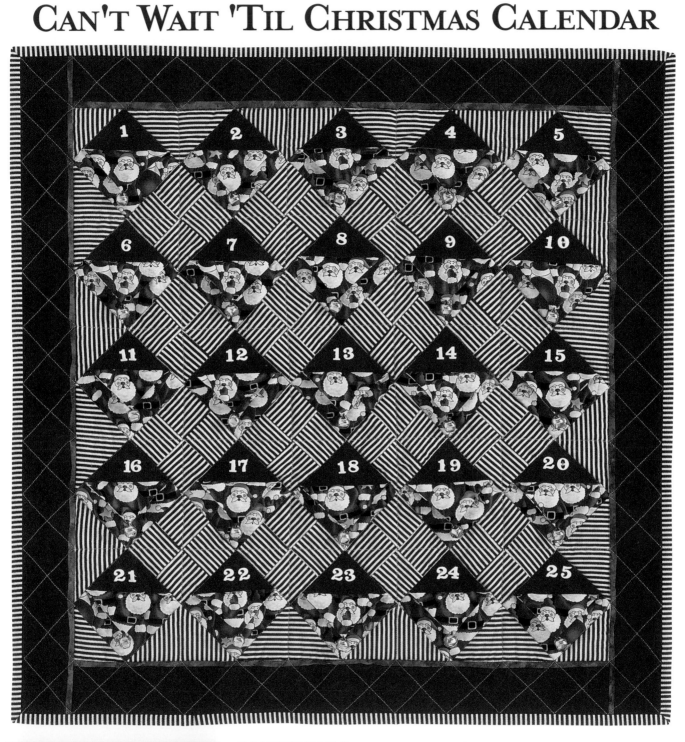

FOLDING TECHNIQUE
- Simple Pockets

CALENDAR
- 25¾" x 25¾"
- 3" finished blocks

MATERIALS

Yardage is based on 42" fabric width.

- ⅝ yard of Christmas print for pockets
- ¾ yard of red print for pocket backgrounds and border
- ¾ yard of small red-and-white stripe for Four-Patch blocks, side and corner setting triangles, and binding
- ⅛ yard of green print for inset strip
- ⅞ yard for backing

- 30" x 30" batting
- 25 jingle bells (12mm)
- Number buttons 1–25 (Resources page 64).
- ¼ yard for hanging sleeve

CUTTING

Always remove selvages.

Christmas Print

- Cut 5 strips 3½" x fabric width. From these strips, cut 50 squares 3½" x 3½" for pockets.

Red Print

- Cut 3 strips 3½" x fabric width. From these strips, cut 25 squares 3½" x 3½" for pocket backgrounds.
- Cut 4 strips 2½" x fabric width for border. (Trim to size later.)

Small Red-and-White Stripe

Follow this cutting order to ensure success.

- Cut 3 strips on the lengthwise grain (parallel to the selvages) 2" x fabric length for Four-Patch blocks.

From the leftover fabric, cut:

- 2 strips on the crosswise grain (90° to the selvages) 2" x fabric width for Four-Patch blocks.
- 2 squares 3" x 3". Cut in half diagonally for corner setting triangles.
- 4 squares 5½" x 5½". Cut in half diagonally twice for setting triangles.
- 4 strips 2¼" x fabric width for binding.

Green Print

- Cut 4 strips 1" x fabric width for inset strip.

Hanging Sleeve

- Cut 1 strip 8" x fabric width for hanging sleeve. (Trim to size later.)

FOLDED UNITS

- Make 25 Simple Pockets following the instructions on page 11.

CONSTRUCTION

Use ¼" seam allowance.

FOUR-PATCH BLOCKS

1. Cut 1 lengthwise strip in half. Sew 1 of the half strips to an end of each of the remaining 2 lengthwise strips.

2. Place 1 crosswise strip and 1 lengthwise strip of the stripe fabric, right sides together.

3. Stitch along 1 long edge. Press either direction. Repeat for the other 2 strips.

4. Trim 1 end of each strip set straight and cut into 32 units 2" wide.

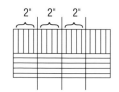

Stitch and cut into 2" units.

5. Stitch 2 of the units into a block. Press. Make 16 blocks.

Stitch.

TOP

1. Place a pocket (design oriented upright) on top of the right side of a background square. Line up the raw edges and baste ⅛" from the raw edges. Make 25 blocks.

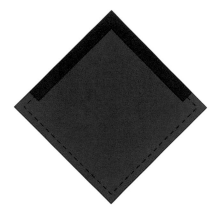

Line up the edges and baste.

2. Arrange the blocks as shown in the illustration.

3. Stitch the blocks into rows. *Be careful not to catch the finished edge of the pockets in the stitched seam.* Press.

4. Stitch the rows together. See note in Step 3. Press.

BORDERS

Your top should measure 21¾" x 21¾". If it does, follow the instructions below and trim the border strips to the lengths specified. If it doesn't, see page 62 for how to measure and trim the border strips to fit your top.

1. Fold each inset strip in half lengthwise and press.

2. Trim 2 of the inset strips to 21¾" long.

3. Trim 2 of the border strips to 21¾" long.

4. Place a short inset strip along the top edge of the quilt top. Place a border strip on top of the inset strip. Align the raw edges and pin. Stitch and press.

5. Repeat for the bottom edge of the quilt top.

6. Trim the other 2 inset strips to 25¾" long.

7. Trim the other 2 border strips to 25¾" long.

8. Layer and pin the other inset strips with the other border strips on the sides of the quilt top. Stitch and press.

FINISHING

QUILTING
1. Layer and baste following the instructions on page 62.

2. Stitch in-the-ditch around the blocks and borders. Quilt diagonally corner to corner through the four-patches and quilt a diagonal grid on the border.

EMBELLISHMENT
1. Stitch the jingle bells to the tips of the pockets.

2. Stitch the number buttons onto the pocket backgrounds.

FINISHING TOUCHES
1. Add binding following the instructions on pages 62–63.

2. Add a hanging sleeve following the instructions on page 63.

3. Be sure to add a label to your Christmas treasure.

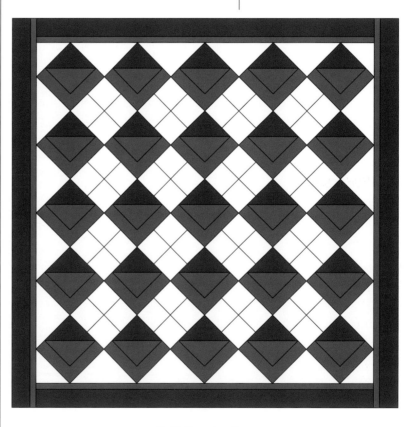

Quilt Construction

VISIONS OF SUGAR PLUMS STOCKING

FOLDING TECHNIQUE
- Folded Squares

STOCKING
- 8" x 16"
- 2" finished blocks

MATERIALS

Yardage is based on 42" fabric width.

- ⅛ yard of plaid for the dividing strips
- ⅞ yard of green plaid for folded squares, pieced blocks, binding, hanger, backing, and lining
- ⅛ yard of small red-and-white stripe for the pieced blocks and folded square inserts
- ⅛ yard of medium red-and-white stripe for the folded square backgrounds
- ⅛ yard of red plaid for the pieced block backgrounds
- 24" x 20" batting
- 15 buttons (¾")
- 20 beads (⅛")

CUTTING

Always remove selvages.

Plaid

- Cut 1 strip 2½" x fabric width for the dividing strips. From this strip, cut 2 strips 2½" x 8½", 1 strip 2½" x 11", and 1 strip 2½" x 8".
- Cut 1 strip 1½" x 8½" for the top dividing strip.

Green Plaid

- Cut 1 strip 4½" x fabric width. From this strip, cut 5 squares 4½" x 4½" for folded squares.
- From the leftover 4½" strip, cut 7 squares 1¾" x 1¾" for pieced blocks.
- Cut 1 strip 2¼" x fabric width for binding and hanger.
- Backing and lining will be cut later.

Small Red-and-White Stripe

- Cut 1 strip 3½" x fabric width. From this strip, cut 7 squares 2½" x 2½" with the stripe running from corner to corner for pieced blocks using the pattern on page 61, then...
- Cut 5 squares 2½" x 2½" for folded square inserts.

Medium Red-and-White Stripe

- Cut 1 strip 2½" x fabric width. From this strip, cut 4 rectangles 2½" x 1¾" for row backgrounds; then...
- Cut 1 rectangle 2½" x 4½" for row backgrounds.

Red Plaid

- Cut 1 strip 4⅛" x fabric width. From this strip, cut 3 squares 4⅛" x 4⅛" for setting triangles. Cut in half diagonally twice.
- From the leftover 4⅛" strip, cut 4 squares 2⅜" x 2⅜". Cut in half diagonally.

FOLDED UNITS

- Make 5 Folded Squares following the instructions on page 16. Place the small red-and-white stripe

inserts into the center of the folded squares. Trim the inserts slightly, if needed, so they lie flat.

CONSTRUCTION

Use ¼" seam allowance.

PIECED BLOCKS

1. Using the illustration as a guide, place a green plaid square on top of a 2½" red-and-white striped square, with right sides together, aligning the top corners. Stitch and trim.

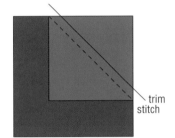
Align top corner, stitch, and trim.

2. Press. Make 7 blocks.

Press.

STOCKING FRONT

1. Stitch the pieced blocks and set-ting triangles into a row as shown. Press. Repeat using 4 pieced blocks. Press.

2. Stitch the folded squares and backgrounds into a row.

3. Trace and complete the stocking pattern on page 61.

4. Arrange the rows and dividing strips, adjusting the placement so they completely cover the pattern.

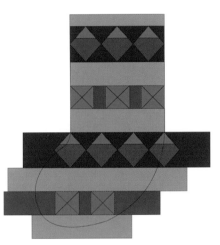
Adjust the rows to cover the pattern.

5. Stitch the rows together. Press.

6. Cut out the stocking using the pattern.

7. Place the lining fabric wrong side up. Lay the batting on top of the lining with the stocking front right side up on top of the batting.

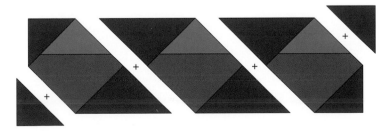
Stitch the row.

Baste the layers together.

8. Stitch in-the-ditch between the rows.

9. Trim around the stocking to remove the extra batting and lining.

STOCKING BACK
1. Layer the backing wrong side up; the batting and the lining right side up. Baste the layers together.

2. Quilt as desired.

3. Using the stocking front as a pattern, cut out the stocking back.

FINISHING

FINISHING TOUCHES
1. With right sides together, stitch the stocking together, leaving the top edge open.

2. Make the folded binding strip following the instructions on page 63 (Step B). Trim off an 18" piece of the folded strip for the binding and an 8" piece for the hanger.

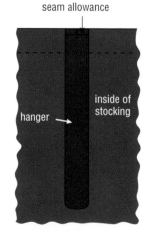

Insert the hanger into the binding seam allowance.

3. Open the 8" piece and fold long raw edges to meet at the center fold line. Fold in half along center fold line. Topstitch along both folded edges.

4. Fold the 8" piece for the hanger in half, matching raw edges. Stitch the binding onto the top edge of the stocking, inserting the hanger (on the inside of the stocking) into the stitching.

5. Hand stitch the binding to the inside of the stocking, leaving the hanger hanging down inside the stocking.

6. Bring the hanger up and hand stitch to secure into position.

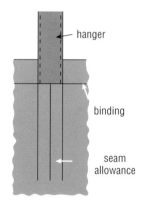

Stitch to secure.

7. Sew on the buttons.

8. Bring each center point of each folded square to the outside edge and secure with a stitched bead.

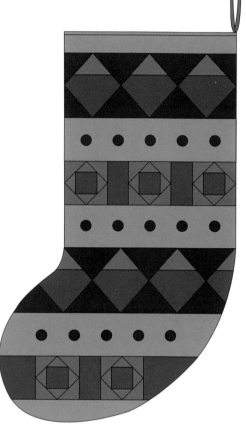

Stocking Construction

An·Elegant·Christmas

CHRISTMAS TREE—ALL DRESSED UP QUILT

FOLDING TECHNIQUES
- **Traditional Prairie Points**
- **Folded Squares**

QUILT
- **48¾" x 50⅞"**
- **3" finished blocks**

MATERIALS

Yardage is based on 42" fabric width.

- ¼ yard each of 7 green prints for folded squares
- 1 yard of green-and-tan print for alternate squares and outer border
- ¼ yard of green print for Four-Patch blocks
- ⅞ yard of burgundy print for Four-Patch blocks, inner border, and binding
- ⅛ yard of brown print for tree trunk
- ¾ yard each of 3 off-white prints for Rail Fence blocks

- ¾ yard of gold lamé for folded square inserts and prairie points
- 3 yards for backing
- 53" x 55" batting
- 56 beads (6mm)
- ½ yard for hanging sleeve

CUTTING

Always remove selvages.

Green Prints

- Cut 2 squares 7" x 7" from each

of the 7 fabrics for folded squares (14 total).

Green-and-Tan Print
- Cut 3 strips 3½" x fabric length on the lengthwise grain. From these strips, cut 32 squares 3½" x 3½" for alternate squares.
- Cut 5 strips 4½" x fabric width for outer border. (Trim to size later.)

Green Print
- Cut 2 strips 2" x fabric width for Four-Patch blocks.

Burgundy Print
- Cut 2 strips 2" x fabric width for Four-Patch blocks.
- Cut 4 strips 1½" x fabric width for inner border. (Trim to size later.)
- Cut 6 strips 2¼" x fabric width for binding.

Brown Print
- Cut 1 strip 3½" x fabric width. From this strip, cut 4 squares 3½" x 3½" for the tree trunk.

Off-White Prints
- Cut 12 strips 1½" x fabric width from each of the 3 fabrics.

Gold Lamé
- Cut 2 strips 3¼" x fabric width. From these strips, cut 14 squares 3¼" x 3¼" for folded square inserts.
- Cut 6 strips 3" x fabric width. From these strips, cut 70 squares 3" x 3" for prairie points.

Hanging Sleeve
- Cut 2 strips 8" x fabric width for hanging sleeve. (Trim to size later.)

FOLDED UNITS

- Make 70 Traditional Prairie Points following the instructions on page 9.
- Make 14 Folded Squares following the instructions on page 16. Place the gold lamé inserts into the center of the folded squares. Trim the inserts slightly if needed so they lie flat.

CONSTRUCTION
Use ¼" seam allowance.

FOUR-PATCH BLOCKS
1. Place 1 green strip and 1 burgundy strip, right sides together.

2. Stitch along 1 long edge. Press. Repeat for the other 2 strips.

3. Trim 1 end of each strip set straight and cut into 26 units 2" wide.

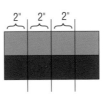

Stitch and cut into 2" units.

4. Stitch 2 of the units into a block. Press. Make 13 blocks.

Stitch.

RAIL FENCE BLOCKS
1. Choose 1 strip of each of the 3 off-white fabrics. With right sides together, stitch 2 strips together along 1 long side. Repeat for the third off-white strip. Press. Repeat for remaining strips, mixing up the order as you stitch the strips together.

2. Trim 1 end of each strip set straight and cut into 129 squares 3½" x 3½".

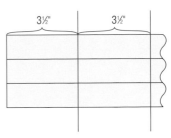

Stitch and cut into 3½" squares.

TOP
1. Place 1 of the brown print squares on top of 1 of the Rail Fence blocks, right sides together. Stitch from corner to corner. Trim and press. Repeat to make 2 blocks.

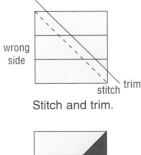

Stitch and trim.

Press.

2. Arrange the blocks as shown in the illustration.

3. Stitch the blocks into diagonal rows. Press.

4. Stitch the rows together. Press.

5. Trim the outside edge of the quilt top as shown.

6. Place 17 overlapping prairie points on the top edge of the quilt top. Baste ⅛" from edge. Repeat for the bottom edge.

7. Place 18 overlapping prairie points on 1 side edge of the quilt top. Baste ⅛" from edge. Repeat for the other side.

BORDERS

Your top should measure 38¾" x 40⅞". If it does, follow the instructions below and trim the border strips to the lengths specified. If it doesn't, see page 62 for how to measure and trim the border strips to fit your top.

Inner Border

1. Trim 2 of the inner border strips to 40⅞" long. Stitch them to the sides. Press.

2. Trim the other 2 inner border strips to 40¾" long. Stitch them to the top and bottom. Press.

Outer Border

1. Stitch the 5 border strips together, end to end, into 1 long strip. From this strip, cut 2 outer border strips 42⅞" long.

2. Stitch them to the sides. Press.

3. From the remaining strips, cut the other 2 outer border strips 48¾" long. Stitch them to the top and bottom. Press.

sew line
trim line

Trim.

FINISHING

QUILTING
1. Layer and baste following the instructions on page 62.

2. Stitch in-the-ditch around the blocks and borders. I stitched a simple swag in the border.

EMBELLISHMENT
Bring each center point of each folded square to the outside edge and secure with a stitched bead.

FINISHING TOUCHES
1. Add binding following the instructions on pages 62–63.

2. Stitch the 2 strips together end to end. Add a hanging sleeve following the instructions on page 63.

3. Be sure to add a label to your Christmas heirloom.

Quilt Construction

COUNTDOWN TO CHRISTMAS CALENDAR

Pockets closed

MATERIALS

Yardage is based on 42" fabric width.

- ¾ yard of burgundy print for pockets
- ¼ yard of gold lamé for pocket backgrounds
- ½ yard of green print for alternate blocks and binding
- ¼ yard of brown print for tree trunk
- ¼ yard each of 4 off-white prints for background squares, side and corner setting triangles
- ¾ yard for backing
- 28" x 29" batting
- 25 gold beads (9 mm)

- Number buttons 1–25 (see Resources page 64)
- 2 yards thin, gold elastic cording
- ¼ yard for hanging sleeve

CUTTING

Always remove selvages.

Burgundy Print
- Cut 4 strips 5" x fabric width. From these strips, cut 25 squares 5" x 5" for pockets.

Gold Lamé
- Cut 2 strips 2½" x fabric width. From these strips, cut 25 squares 2½" x 2½" for pocket backgrounds.

Green Print
- Cut 3 strips 2½" x fabric width. From these strips, cut 34 squares 2½" x 2½" for alternate blocks.
- Cut 3 strips 2¼" x fabric width for binding.

Brown Print
- Cut 3 squares 2½" x 2½" for tree trunk.
- Cut 1 square 4⅛" x 4⅛". Cut in half diagonally twice for tree trunk setting triangle.

Off-White Prints
- Cut 1 strip 2½" x fabric width from each of the 4 fabrics. From these strips, cut 58 squares 2½" x for background.

- Cut 1 square 2⅜" x 2⅜". Cut in half diagonally for bottom corner setting triangles.
- Cut 1 strip 4⅛" x fabric width. From this strip, cut 8 squares 4⅛" x 4⅛". Cut in half diagonally twice for setting triangles.

Hanging Sleeve
- Cut 1 strip 8" x fabric width for hanging sleeve. (Trim to size later.)

Pockets open

FOLDED UNITS

- Make 25 Pockets with Fold following the instructions on page 12.

CONSTRUCTION

Use ¼" seam allowance.

TOP

1. Place a pocket (folded side on top) on the right side of a pocket background square. Line up the raw edges and baste ⅛" from edge. Make

14 blocks. Repeat for the remaining 11 blocks, except place the pocket (plain side on top) on the right side of the pocket background square.

Place folded side on top, line up the edges, and baste.

Place plain side on top, line up the edges, and baste.

2. Place 1 of the brown print squares on top of 1 of the 2½" off-white background squares, right sides together. Stitch from corner to corner. Trim and press. Repeat to make 2 blocks.

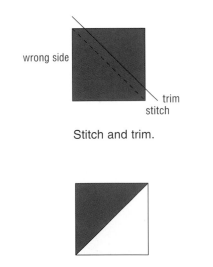

wrong side

trim
stitch

Stitch and trim.

Press.

3. Arrange the blocks following the illustration.

4. Stitch the blocks into rows. *Be careful not to catch the folded edge of the pockets in the stitched seam.* Press.

5. Stitch the rows together. See note in Step 3. Press.

FINISHING

QUILTING
1. Layer and baste following the instructions on page 62.

2. Stitch in-the-ditch around the blocks.

EMBELLISHMENT
1. Stitch the gold beads to the tips of the pockets.

2. Stitch the number buttons onto the pockets. Stitch through only the pocket, not through all of the layers, or you won't be able to put anything in the pockets.

3. Stitch a loop of gold elastic cording at the bottom corner of each pocket and at the top corners of each pocket background. This will enable you to fasten the pockets either open or closed. To do this, bring the needle up from the back of the quilt, then back down through the front of the quilt, returning to the back. Leave a small loop on the front of the quilt and tie

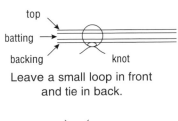

top
batting
backing
knot

Leave a small loop in front and tie in back.

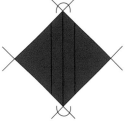

Add loops to the top and bottom of each pocket.

off the elastic on the back. Trim off the elastic and continue.

FINISHING TOUCHES
1. Add binding following the instructions on pages 62–63.

2. Add a hanging sleeve following the instructions on page 63.

3. Be sure to add a label to your treasure.

Quilt Construction

FOLDED-SQUARE PILLOW

FOLDING TECHNIQUE
- Folded Square

PILLOW
- 16" x 16"

MATERIALS
Yardage is based on 42" fabric width.

- 1⅜ yards of burgundy print for folded square and pillow backing
- ⅜ yard of green print for folded square insert
- ⅜ yard of white print for folded square insert
- 18" pillow form (for a tightly stuffed pillow)
- 8 buttons (four 1", four 1¼")

CUTTING

Always remove selvages.

Burgundy Print

- Cut 1 square 33" x 33" for folded square.
- Cut 1 strip 11" x fabric width on crosswise grain (90° to selvages). From this strip, cut 2 rectangles 11" x 16½" for pillow backing.

Green Print

- Cut 1 square 12" x 12" for folded square insert. Cut in half diagonally.

White Print

- Cut 1 square 12" x 12" for folded square insert. Cut in half diagonally.

FOLDED UNITS

- Make 1 Folded Square following the instructions on page 16.

CONSTRUCTION

Use ¼" seam allowance.

FOLDED SQUARE INSERT

Stitch the triangles together as shown. Press. *The outer edges are on the bias, so be careful not to stretch them. They will be stabilized when enclosed in seams.*

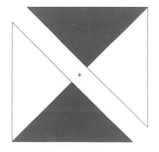

Stitch triangles.

PILLOW TOP

Place the insert into the folded square. Trim the insert slightly, if needed, so it lies flat. Stitch in-the-ditch to secure the layers.

PILLOW BACKING

Fold under ¼" twice on 1 long edge of 1 of the pillow backing rectangles. Stitch. Repeat for the other pillow backing rectangle.

PILLOW CONSTRUCTION

Place the pillow top right side up. Place the pillow backing rectangles wrong side up, matching the 16½" sides and overlapping in the center, as shown. Stitch around the edge.

Place backing on pillow top and stitch.

FINISHING

1. Bring each center point of the folded square to the outside edge and secure with a 1¼" button.

2. Smooth the folded square and secure each inner corner with a 1" button.

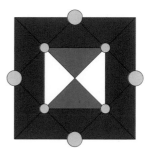

Add buttons.

3. Insert the pillow form.

·A·Classic· Christmas

FOLDED CHINESE COINS QUILT

FOLDING TECHNIQUE
- Rectangle Origami Puffs

QUILT
- 41½" x 48½"
- 4" x 2" finished rectangles

MATERIALS
Yardage is based on 42" fabric width.

- ¼ yard each of 10 red prints for rectangle origami puffs

- ¼ yard each of 10 green prints for rectangle origami puffs
- ⅞ yard of black-and-green print for dividing strips and binding
- ¼ yard of red-and-gold print for inner border

- ⅝ yard of dark green print for outer border
- ¼ yard for folding foundations
- 1⅝ yards for backing
- 46" x 53" batting
- ¼ yard for hanging sleeve

CUTTING

Always remove selvages.

Red Prints
- Cut 1 strip 3½" x fabric width from each fabric. From each strip, cut 5 rectangles 3½" x 5½" for rectangle origami puffs.

Green Prints
- Cut 1 strip 3½" x fabric width from each fabric. From each strip, cut 5 rectangles 3½" x 5½" for rectangle origami puffs.

Black-and-Green Print
- Cut 4 strips 3½" x fabric width for dividing strips. From these strips, cut 4 strips 3½" x 39½".
- Cut 5 strips 2¼" x fabric width for binding.

Red-and-Gold Print
- Cut 4 strips 1½" x fabric width for inner border. (Trim to size later.)

Dark Green Print
- Cut 4 strips 4" x fabric width for outer border. (Trim to size later.)

Foundations
- Cut 1 strip 4½" x fabric width. From this strip, cut 10 rectangles 2½" x 4½".

Hanging Sleeve
- Cut 1 strip 8" x fabric width for hanging sleeve. (Trim to size later.)

FOLDED UNITS

- Make 100 Rectangle Origami Puffs following the instructions on page 15.

CONSTRUCTION
Use ¼" seam allowance.

TOP
1. Arrange the blocks as shown in the illustration, alternating red, green, red, green, and so on.

2. Stitch the blocks into rows. Press.

3. Trim 1" off the end green block in each row as shown.

4. Stitch the rows and dividing strips together. Press.

BORDERS
Your top should measure 32½" x 39½". If it does, follow the instructions below and trim the border strips to the lengths specified. If it doesn't, see page 62 for how to measure and trim the border strips to fit your top.

Inner Border
1. Trim 2 of the inner border strips to 39½" long. Stitch them to the sides. Press.

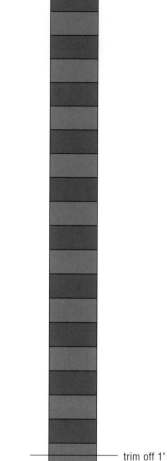

trim off 1"

Trim the last green block in each row.

2. Trim the other 2 inner border strips to 34½" long. Stitch them to the top and bottom. Press.

Outer Border
1. Trim 2 of the outer border strips to 41½" long. Stitch them to the sides. Press.

2. Trim the other 2 outer border strips to 41½" long. Stitch them to the top and bottom. Press.

FINISHING

QUILTING

1. Layer and baste following the instructions on page 62.

2. Stitch in-the-ditch around the blocks and borders. Channel-quilt the dividing strips and borders.

FINISHING TOUCHES

1. Add binding following the instructions on pages 62–63.

2. Add a hanging sleeve following the instructions on page 63.

3. Be sure to add a label to your Christmas heirloom.

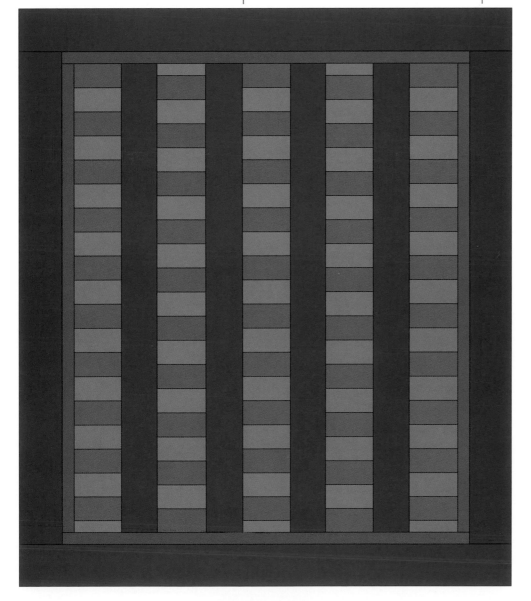

Quilt Construction

CHRISTMASTIME
TABLE RUNNER AND PLACEMATS

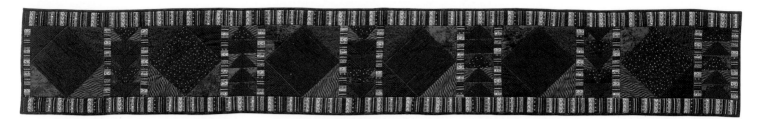

FOLDING TECHNIQUES
- **Double Tucks**
- **Prairie Points with Fold**

TABLE RUNNER
- **97½" x 14½"**

PLACEMAT
- **17½" x 14½"**

MATERIALS

Yardage is based on 42" fabric width. These requirements are for one table runner OR six placemats.

- ⅔ yard each of 3 red prints for the double tucked squares and prairie points
- ¼ yard of 4 green prints for setting triangles and prairie points backgrounds
- ¾ yard of stripe for dividing strip and borders
- 1⅝ yards of backing for table runner OR placemats
- ½ yard of green print for table runner binding OR ⅞ yard for placemat binding

- 19" x 102" batting for table runner OR 6 pieces 19" x 22" for placemats

CUTTING
Always remove selvages.

Red Prints
- Cut 1 strip 9" x fabric width from each red print for the double tucked squares.
- Cut 2 strips 4½" x fabric width

from each fabric. From these strips, cut 10 rectangles 4½" x 5" (30 total) from each fabric for the prairie points.

Green Prints
- Cut 1 strip 6" x fabric width from each fabric. From each strip, cut 3 squares 6" x 6", then cut in half diagonally for setting triangles. From the remainder, cut 8 rectangles 2½" x 4½" from each fabric

for the prairie point backgrounds (30 total).

- Cut 7 strips 2¼" x fabric width for table runner binding.

OR

- Cut 12 strips 2¼" x fabric width for placemat binding.

Stripe

- Cut 5 strips 2½" x fabric width for top and bottom borders of table runner. Stitch these strips into a long strip. From this strip, cut 2 strips 97½" long.
- Cut 4 strips 1½" x fabric width for dividing strips and side borders for table runner. From each strip, cut 4 strips 10½" long (13 total).

OR

- Cut 6 strips 2½" x fabric width for top and bottom borders for placemats. From each strip, cut 2 strips 17½" long (12 total).
- Cut 5 strips 1½" x fabric width for dividing strips and side borders for placemats. From each strip, cut 4 strips 10½" long (18 total).

FOLDED UNITS

- Make 4 Double Tucks per strip following the instructions on pages 8–9. From each of the double tucked strips, cut 2 squares 7⅝" x 7⅝". Be sure there are 2 Double Tucks centered in the square.
- Make 30 Prairie Points with Fold following the instructions on page 10.

CONSTRUCTION

Use ¼" seam allowance.

CENTER SQUARE BLOCKS

1. Stitch 2 green triangles to opposite sides of a double-tucked square.

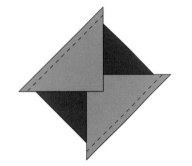

Stitch triangles to opposite sides of a tucked square.

2. Press open and add 2 more green triangles to the other opposite sides.

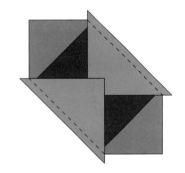

Repeat for 2 more triangles.

3. Press open. Repeat to make 6 blocks.

Make 6 blocks.

PRAIRIE POINT BLOCKS

1. Baste a prairie point to one long edge of a green rectangle ⅛" from edge. Repeat for all 30 units.

Baste prairie points to the rectangles.

2. Stitch 5 prairie point units together. Repeat to make 6 blocks.

Stitch units together.

TOP

1. Arrange the blocks and dividing strips following the illustrations.

2. Stitch the blocks and dividing strips together. *Notice that the prairie point blocks and double-tucked blocks alternate direction on the table runner.* Press.

BORDER

Your top should measure 95½" x 10½" OR 15½" x 10½". If it does, follow the instructions below and trim the border strips to the lengths specified. If it doesn't, see page 62 for how to measure and trim the border strips to fit your top.

1. Stitch a 10½" strip to each short side of either the table runner OR each placemat. Press.

2. Stitch the two 97½" strips to the top and bottom of the table runner OR stitch two 17½" strips to the top and bottom of each placemat. Press.

FINISHING

1. Layer and baste following the instructions on page 62.

2. Stitch in-the-ditch around the pieces and borders.

3. Add binding following the instructions on pages 62–63.

Placemat Construction

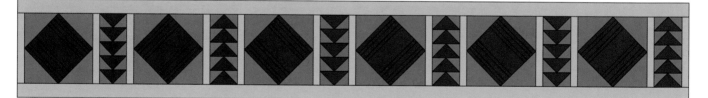

Table Runner Construction

FOLDED EIGHT-POINTED STAR PILLOW

MATERIALS

Yardage is based on 42" fabric width.

- 8½" x 8½" of gold lamé for eight-pointed star
- ⅝ yard of stripe for folded eight-pointed star background and pillow backing
- 5" x 10" of green print for corners
- ⅝ yard of red print for borders
- ½ yard for pillow top backing
- 18" x 18" batting
- 18" pillow form (for a tightly stuffed pillow)
- 40–44 gold beads (6 mm)

CUTTING

Always remove selvages.

Gold Lamé
- Cut 1 square 8½" square for eight-pointed star.

Stripe
- Cut 1 strip 11" x fabric width. From this strip, cut 2 rectangles 11" x 16½" for pillow backing.
- Cut 1 square 6¼" x 6¼" for eight-pointed star background.

Green Print
- Cut 2 squares 5" x 5". Cut in half diagonally for corners.

Red Print
- Cut 4 strips 4½" x fabric width for borders.

Pillow Top Backing
- Cut 1 square 18" x 18".

FOLDED UNITS

- Make 1 Folded Eight-Pointed Star following the instructions on pages 17–22.
- Make 4 border strips with Single Tucks following the instructions on pages 6–7.

CONSTRUCTION

Use ¼" seam allowance.

PILLOW TOP

1. Appliqué the folded eight-pointed star onto the stripe background.

2. Stitch a green corner triangle onto each side of the stripe background. Press.

3. Trim the border strips to 12½" long. *When you trim the single-tucked border strip, adjust where you cut to allow an untucked section for the seam allowance. Remove the stitching of one tuck if necessary.*

4. Place the first border strip on 1 edge of the pillow top. Stitch part way down the length of the border.

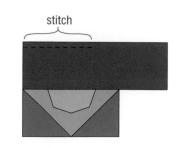

stitch

Stitch part way down the first border.

5. Stitch the second border to the pillow top. Repeat for the remaining 2 borders.

Stitch the other borders.

6. Finish stitching the first border. Press.

7. Layer the pillow top backing wrong side up; the batting and the pillow top right side up. Baste and stitch in-the-ditch around the folded eight-pointed star, background, and borders.

PILLOW BACKING

Fold under ¼" twice on 1 long edge of 1 of the pillow backing rectangles. Stitch. Repeat for the other pillow backing rectangle.

PILLOW CONSTRUCTION

Place the pillow top right side up. Place the pillow backing rectangles wrong side up, matching the 16½" sides and overlapping in the center, as shown. Stitch around the edge.

Place backing on pillow top and stitch.

FINISHING

1. Tack the tucks as shown.

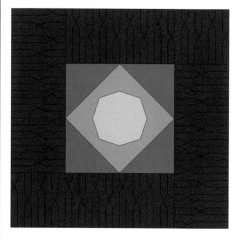

Tacked tucks.

2. Stitch the gold beads to the 4 center points of the folded eight-pointed star and to the tucks and corners of the borders.

3. Insert the pillow form.

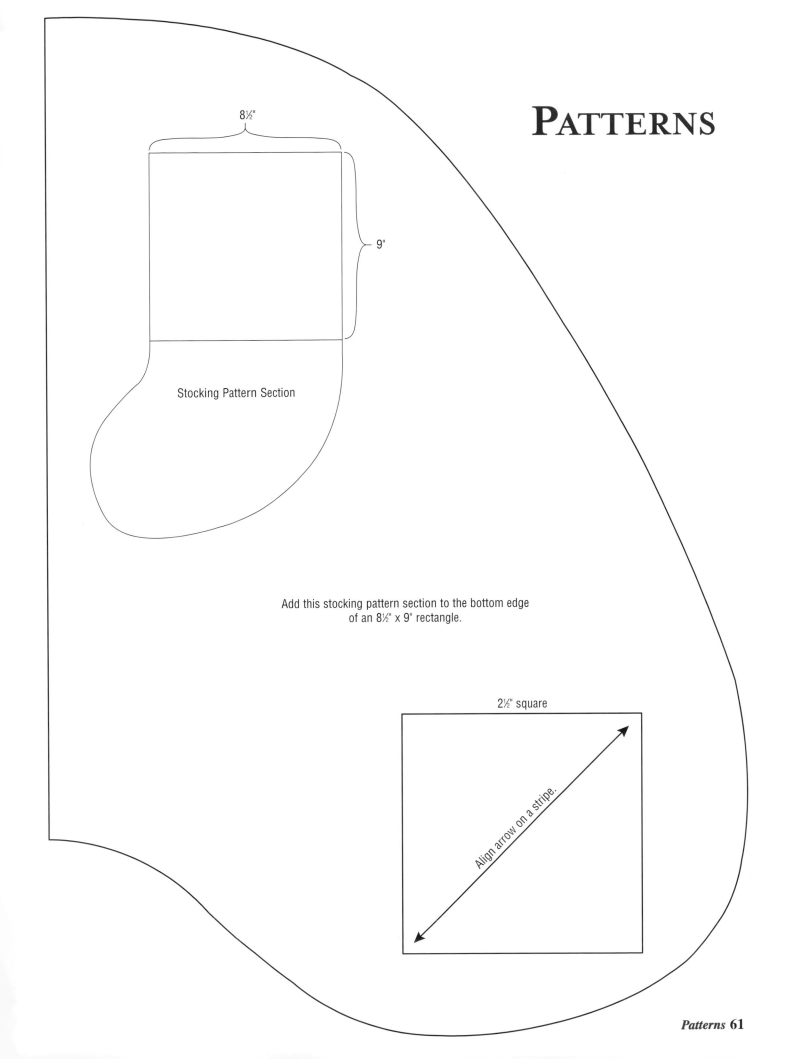

PATTERNS

8½"

9"

Stocking Pattern Section

Add this stocking pattern section to the bottom edge
of an 8½" x 9" rectangle.

2½" square

Align arrow on a stripe.

Quilting Basics

Fabrics

Fabric requirements are based on a 42" fabric width. Fabrics that are 100% cotton work best; they hold a crease well for the folding. Whether to prewash or not is a personal choice. If you choose not to prewash, at least check to be sure that the fabrics you choose will not bleed—reds are especially suspect.

Seam Allowances

Use a ¼" seam allowance. It's a good idea to do a test seam before you begin stitching to check that your ¼" is accurate.

Pressing

Press the seam allowances away from the folded units. Press pieced units lightly in an up-and-down motion. I use steam and moderate pressure when pressing the folded units.

Borders

1. Press the quilt top well.

2. Measure the quilt top vertically across the center. Cut 2 strips this length for the side borders.

3. Place pins at the centers of all four sides of the quilt top, as well as in the center of each side border strip. Pin the side borders to the quilt top matching the center pins.

4. Using a ¼" seam allowance, stitch the borders to the quilt top and press.

5. Measure the quilt top horizontally across the center, including the side borders. Cut 2 strips this length for the top and bottom borders. Repeat pinning, stitching, and pressing.

Backing

Cut the backing at least 2" larger than the quilt top on all sides. Prewash the fabric, if desired, and trim off the selvages.

Batting

Cut the batting approximately 2" larger than your quilt top on all sides.

Layering

1. Spread the backing wrong side up and tape the edges down with masking tape. If you are working on carpet you can use T-pins to secure the backing to the carpet.

2. Center the batting on top, smoothing out any wrinkles.

3. Center the quilt top, right side up, on top of the batting and backing.

Basting

If you plan to machine quilt, pin-baste the quilt layers together with safety pins placed a minimum of 3"–4" apart. Begin basting in the center and move toward the edges first in vertical, then horizontal, rows.

If you plan to hand quilt, baste the layers together with thread using a long needle and light-colored thread. Knot one end of the thread. Using stitches approximately the length of the needle, begin in the center and move out toward the edges.

Quilting

Quilting, whether by hand or machine, enhances the design of the quilt. You may choose to quilt in-the-ditch, echo the pieced or appliqué motifs, use patterns from quilting design books and stencils, or do your own free-motion quilting. Quilting suggestions are included in the projects.

Binding

1. Trim excess batting and backing from the quilt. If you want a ¼" finished binding, cut the strips 2¼" wide and stitch them together with diagonal seams to make a continuous binding strip.

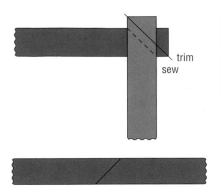

2. Press the seams open, then press the entire strip in half lengthwise with wrong sides together.

3. With raw edges even, start pinning the binding to the edge of the quilt a few inches away from one corner, leaving the first few inches of the binding unattached.

4. Stitch using a ¼" seam allowance. Stop stitching ¼" away from the first corner (Step A), backstitch one stitch.

Step A. Stitch to ¼" from corner.

5. Remove the quilt from the machine and trim off the threads.

6. Rotate the quilt. Fold the binding at a right angle so it extends straight above the quilt (Step B), forming a 45° fold.

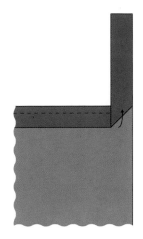

Step B. First fold for miter

7. Bring the binding strip down even with the edge of the quilt (Step C). Begin sewing at the folded edge.

Step C. Second fold alignment

8. Repeat in the same manner at all corners.

9. Finish the binding by folding the beginning end ¼" and overlapping it with the ending end, trimming off any leftover binding.

10. Fold the binding over to the back of the quilt and blindstitch the binding to the backing.

HANGING SLEEVE

1. Cut number of strips indicated in project directions 8" x fabric width. If more than 1 strip is cut, stitch strips together. Press seam open. Measure top width of project. Trim strip to this measurement.

2. Fold ¼" of 1 short edge. Fold a second time. Press and stitch to finish the edge. Repeat for the other short edge.

3. With wrong sides together, match the 2 long raw edges and stitch.

4. Turn right side out. Press with the seam down the center of one side.

Press.

5. Position the sleeve along the top edge of the back of the quilt and hand stitch. Be sure your stitches do not go all the way through to the front of the quilt.

Resources

For quilting supplies (including 1–25 number buttons):
Cotton Patch Mail Order
3405 Hall Lane, Dept. CTB
Lafayette, CA 94549
(800) 835-4418
(925) 283-7883
email: quiltusa@yahoo.com
website: www.quiltusa.com
Note: *Fabrics used in the quilts shown may not be currently available because fabric manufacturers keep most fabrics in print for only a short time.*

For information about other C&T books, write for a free catalog:
C&T Publishing, Inc.
P.O. Box 1456
Lafayette, CA 94549
(800) 284-1114
email: ctinfo@ctpub.com
website: www.ctpub.com

Index

About the Author

Liz has been quilting since 1981. Her love of quilting began when she took her first class to have something creative to do while she stayed home with her two young daughters. This class opened the world of fabric and quilting to her. She enjoys trying new techniques that extend just beyond basic traditional quilting.

She lives in California with her husband; her two almost-grown daughters are not far away.